Praise for Lent

"I didn't think I'd forgotten how close poetry can get to us—inside our eyes, below our thoughts—but reading Kate Cayley's poems, I feel newly awed at their sure and profound nearness."
—Sadiqa de Meijer, Governor General's Literary Award–winning author of *alfabet/alphabet*

"Eventually, most of the things one loves fill one with worry, and, paradoxically, the more deeply one loves, the more quickly one is filled. Poetry fills me with worry—because, thankfully, it is always changing. But Kate Cayley's *Lent*, though it is filled with love and worry, doesn't worry me at all—not because it isn't new; it's as new as tomorrow—but because it is so well made. These are poems that are completed by their encounters with difficult things—they do not take note of, they live with. And they read the way the best poems do, like parts of one returned to one. I love this book; it does not worry me."
—Shane McCrae, author of *Cain Named the Animal*

"Gorgeous and startling, the poems in Kate Cayley's *Lent* emerge as a testament to poetry itself: the desire to grapple with an imperfect world, and yet respond with praise. 'Show me/the pith of my own heart,' she writes, despite the darkness. These are poems filled with hope, searingly intelligent, by one of our country's finest poets. *Lent* is a wonder."
—Steven Price, Scotiabank Giller Prize–shortlisted author of *Lampedusa*

Additional Praise for Kate Cayley

"Beware of Kate Cayley. With an agility stolen from some other world she flicks this one open and invites us to watch our certainties scuttling away."
—Martha Baillie, author of *If Clara*

"Kate Cayley is splendid in her deft arrangement of the sentence, and in her depiction of the quotidian but just askew enough to be new and surprising."
—Kerry Clare, *Pickle Me This*

"This writer's a winner—in more ways than one."
—Susan G. Cole, *NOW Magazine*

"Cayley's world is a dangerous place, all the structures built with discarded slivering wood and rusted nails, but one where strange sacredness arrives in the middle of the ordinary day. The mysterious reasons that push her misplaced, displaced people are as convincing as memories, painful but necessary to relive."
—Marina Endicott, author of *The Difference*

"Cayley shows us that the impulse to collect and then work through anxiety imaginatively is important and powerful."
—Michelle Fost, *Cleaver Magazine*

"Kate Cayley explores the circus that is the human heart and proves it to be wild and eccentric, big and sometimes aching, often bursting with wisdom."
—Lisa Moore, author of *This is How We Love*

"Taut and brimming with clarity."
—Souvankham Thammavongsa, Scotiabank Giller Prize–winning author of *How to Pronounce Knife*

Lent

Kate Cayley

Book*hug Press
Toronto 2023

FIRST EDITION

© 2023 by Kate Cayley

Library and Archives Canada Cataloguing in Publication

Title: Lent / Kate Cayley.
Names: Cayley, Kate, author.
Description: Poems.
Identifiers: Canadiana (print) 20220457808 | Canadiana (ebook) 20220457816
    ISBN 9781771668118 (softcover)
    ISBN 9781771668132 (PDF)
    ISBN 9781771668125 (EPUB)
Classification: LCC PS8605.A945 L46 2023 | DDC C811/.6—dc23

The production of this book was made possible through the generous assistance of the Canada Council for the Arts and the Ontario Arts Council. Book*hug Press also acknowledges the support of the Government of Canada through the Canada Book Fund and the Government of Ontario through the Ontario Book Publishing Tax Credit and the Ontario Book Fund.

 Canada Council for the Arts   Conseil des Arts du Canada    ONTARIO ARTS COUNCIL / CONSEIL DES ARTS DE L'ONTARIO / an Ontario government agency / un organisme du gouvernement de l'Ontario

 Canada    ONTARIO CREATES | ONTARIO CRÉATIF

Book*hug Press acknowledges that the land on which we operate is the traditional territory of many nations, including the Mississaugas of the Credit, the Anishnabeg, the Chippewa, the Haudenosaunee, and the Wendat peoples. We recognize the enduring presence of many diverse First Nations, Inuit, and Métis peoples and are grateful for the opportunity to meet and work on this territory.

For Lea

Contents

Interior

Sixty Harvests

Lent

Interior

Attention

And if repetition could itself be
a form of attention, folding along the crease
until the crease finds itself
hollowing out the groove, as in marriage,
studying the same face, the same
permeable body, as in children, their fury, their
fraught going-forward thinning out your life
like a membrane that will not break, lives
that alter in the telling, theirs outstripping yours
and stripping you of anything they find useful yet
carrying you always with them, a husk pinned to their inside
pockets, as the poet who wrote on the back of recipe cards
attended sternly to the rising bread, attended to each
blade of grass on her Amherst lawn, then I will
believe that language first rose up in us
as praise.

Ice Sheet

The ice

at our doorstep thinned

to skin as the sun

broke over it, it breaks

under his small damply booted foot.

Transfixed, he sits.

Look, he says, not

looking up, look.

I am too busy.

The door shuts gently. When

in remorse I open it again, there

he is looking at the ice, which glass

only imitates. He is

secretive in his reverent

curiosity, face bent

out of my sight.

The frozen puddle vast

as the ice over the earth,

which once, perhaps,

we all crossed.

The Dream of Bodies

My mother calls me into the house. The house
is an earthwork. I don't really know
what that is, but walls of sod cuts
drape over a timbered frame and let in a little light.
The sod, studded with dead grass, hangs like
pelts that won't dry. We're looking for the body of my father.

This earthwork is a body-house. The bodies, preserved,
do not sprout or soften. There are many.
When I was a child my mother sorted
Lego bricks into piles, and it's the same here. An impatient
shove to this side, that side. The thing she needs unfound.

There are no familiar bodies, though each is
reminiscent of someone, like a neighbour
I can't put a name to. We keep on. I wonder

if there is a better way to do this: a pause
we owe these departed, a more efficient system?
My father enters, bending at the low doorway.
He is not dead. He was only travelling. We look up,
interrupted. The brightness behind him indicates
it is already day. Neither of us knows how to stop.

Even now, we are guilty, offering
our dusty hands. Are we released?

Objects

I must praise household objects.
For they conquer time patiently
by the sink or door.
For they remember and will not give up secrets.
Toothbrush, scrubbing brush, aluminum lip
of the coffee pot. The spoon, cup
with the cracked handle.
The vacuum pensive under the stairs.
The umbrella with its broken spoke. Faithful
even when cursed or forgotten.
Their bodies, if not their uses, outlast us,
and they do not boast.

Falling

I was putting off God. A task crossed out
each night like laying aside clothing
I can't find time to repair.

My children speak to me from the next room
and I pursue their voices through the house.

I walk my son to the drugstore to buy hoops
for his ears. There's an old man in the doorway

and I give him less than I've spent on the earrings.
My son begins to walk home

in the opposite direction. He is old enough.
The man calls after me *do not lose him.*

When my son was three, the garbage truck driver tied
a loop of string to the handle of the truck's horn

and let him pull it. I don't know what to hope for
except that he will be blessed

with unnecessary kindness, offer it in kind.
He disappears at the corner.

I was still putting off God. The sky began
the ritual of evening and I walked
more quickly, refusing.

Stone Wall

Lichen, rustle of grass. Hands
that briefly rest, then lift. Ghosts.

Blood from stones, bones
knitting.

Ladybug, Bratislava

My father-in-law has, as our son puts it, zero legs. A lifetime of cigarettes,
Soviet defections, marital defections, and now he is shortened, spinning
via his newish wheels to our daughter, who has asked him what a Jew is,
something we have told her she is, without explanation. He parses
ethnicity, identity, history, faith, as her face takes on the polite
absence girls learn early, smiling toward the voice that does not notice
the listener is real, and seven.

Our son shoots the waiter with an imaginary gun
and we shush, invoke good behaviour, which is less strenuous
than virtue and all we have the strength for. He shoots
again. My wife's smile is our daughter's.

In this country we are unmarried and do not touch
even our fingertips. I gag on the coffee,
spit what I hope is a pebble onto the napkin.

Brittle winged insect, intact, dead.

Your house is on fire, your children are gone. Our daughter, glad
of an excuse, carries it outside. The Danube is disappointingly grey,
slicks past a bridge under construction and a mall. Through the window
I see her lay it in the flowerbed and stand back
as if it will fly away.

Toy Rabbit

The small brown rabbit sat on the lower shelf of a Goodwill.

It may be assumed that a child was overcome with longing for the rabbit but lost interest and it became another plastic object painfully underfoot.

Childhood is a time of inexplicable passions. The genius or religious fanatic is tepid compared to the disastrous loves experienced by children.

Their loves are outsized to their objects, and rehearse the squandering of their souls on what is unworthy.

This rabbit is an example of kitsch.

Kitsch is a loanword from German.

The study of kitsch was once extensive in Germany, and notably pursued by Walter Benjamin, who committed suicide in Spain by swallowing morphine tablets after being told he would be returned to Nazi-occupied France.

The other refugees in his party were granted exit visas the next morning, which makes his death especially poignant, or bleakly comic, depending on one's frame of mind.

There are other theories and accounts of his death, which I will not enter into.

Kitsch is easily pressed into service by political ideologies. Fascism, capitalism, and communism have all relied heavily on kitsch.

This seems a lot to blame the rabbit for.

Kitsch is a way to dilute life, and thus bear to go on living.

And the child? Does the child still think of the rabbit?

Walking

When the branches on the bare tree ahead turn to a red mist.

When the slanted stones rising from the water at your right
are a flock of crying birds.

When the pavement on which you set your feet is black ice.
You fall. The pavement will not yield
but offers two consolations:

that you are not yet dead. That you will die.

When the styrofoam granules of snow on the path melt
under your hand.

When some don't. They are styrofoam.

When you recognize the recessed bark of the winter tree
but can't remember its name.

When the orange spangled in the thicket is not plastic
but berries.

When the lake scalloped with light
is the light you saw
as a child walking in the park
when you fell to your knees

embarrassed by how inadequate you were
to what you must praise.

Blue Houses

I have dreamed of blue houses, dreamed

I seek the blue house
that is smallest, smaller

than the house the old woman shuffles to
in her slippers. She wears a housedress
blotched with blue roses. She speaks Polish
in the direction of her neighbour, who doesn't

answer. She will soon die. I will become
an old woman and clutch a wheeled cart.
I will become an exemplar of something
vanishing, and go into the blue house.

Haunting

Who is to be sacrificed?

Is it germane, to contemplate sacrifice?

Must there always be a sacrifice?

Is this question the older, other god's?

Who possesses whom, and how?

Who is the figure in the landscape?

Seen in passing once only?

Is the older, other god

seated in the empty room?

Who will carry the blindfold?

Who will hold the small knife?

Who brought the matches

to meet the straw?

Art Monsters

Assia Wevill Considers Herself [1]

1. Of Sylvia and Turning On the Gas

A blond woman regards me,
intrusive as a cut that bleeds
more than should be possible.
What should be inside is out.

On the kitchen table, four fingers
of whisky, powdered pills.
I dragged in the mattress, laid down
my daughter's bird-bones. She
sleeps through anything. The woman
stares, scorning: my suffering
comparable only, lessened, less.

Nothing here is mine. I've used her leavings,
fitted my hands into her rubber gloves,
her relinquished scissors.

She knows that for me nothing worked
and this pleases her.

But didn't I cross borders, pursued by soldiers?
And mine weren't metaphors. I was
a real Jew. I suppose the figurative flight's
remembered best.

That's life, it seems, or death.

2. *She Works in Advertising*

Ad copy paid for itself. I was good
at sitting with a cigarette, taglines pencilled
onto napkins, creased envelopes. Casual
and easy, to prove I believed in what
we were selling, everything easy

from here on, happiness proliferating,
swinging open like a souvenir chocolate box.

Bare tables banished to childhood,
the glass and gravel picked out of our
wounds, no scars, only
hairdryers, dinner sets, vacations. No
second thoughts. No past.

3. The Sixties

You little fools. I will not give up stockings, or believe
that enlightenment thrives on squalor.
If I lie down and unzip it is a concession and I refuse
to be seen *naturally*. Baubles break, patchouli
gives me headaches, one man is enough. I already have
my hands full with dream interpretation.
Chemical visions would
put me under for good. I pity these unshaven
waifs proffering flowers, babbling the names of god
but forgetting the devil's. He grins in the stove's
blue flame and lies in wait, unzipped.

4. Abortion

The man they found for me was dapper,
suited like a funeral director, discreet as a pinch of salt.
He told me not to sleep as if it were common
for women to doze off as he scraped
out what could have been. It came away in clots,
each a useless heart. I didn't ask myself what I wanted
and no one else thought to. I threw fits
at parties, tore rugs with my teeth, and that
was only to be expected of a woman, so
beautiful, so sad. I lied. Made operas
out of leftovers and revelations from stray remarks
so no one would suspect I would grow old,
a hausfrau in a flowered dress, I guess. My mother was.
I'd sidestepped that briefly. But
ended up on this table nonetheless.

5. Tarot Cards

He told me they often read the cards together, a hint
I would not take. Let Sylvia be the Empress or the Hanged Man. I am
my own archetype, far more exhausting. He was the Magician:
druidic, arms raised, calling to gods not mine. His face pinked, piqued.
The sorrow of the man who holds the knife, nothing is equal to it!
The general who razes the village is monumental
in his guilt, the villagers walk-ons
in his tragedy (like her, I am lavish with metaphors). When he left
I bought a deck. Thought of my parents, their staid
and stubborn disbeliefs, as I spread the cards over the floor. The fool
wears green and yellow, sings as he prances to the cliff edge, dog
following, trying to warn him. My parents were getters-on,
un-ghettoed, and they snorted at anyone in bells.
I heard the little dog yapping at my heels.

6. She Imagines Sylvia Trying to Write

She checks in to a hotel room
sure someone will come after her.

No one does.

The bed is hard. Lumpy.
The windows don't open.

Just the desk,
glowering.

7. She Reads Sylvia's Poetry

She was plausible as a volcano, raining down hot ash until everyone surrendered and agreed. *Every woman adores a Fascist.* If I'd said that, I'd have been ridiculous, laughed at. I'm not strong enough. Even after her death I envied her capacious appetite, how she hamstrung her prisoners, made them look at her face until it was a mirror. If only I could do that. If only.

8. In Which Sylvia Has a Vision of the Animals as She Turns On the Gas

They snuffle wet-nosed at the door, the towels
she's laid do not keep them out.
Black-muzzled dogs, jackboot signature
baying at the moon. Rabbits that menace, prancing,

vanishing at last over the hill of her mind. The deer
with slender faces of warning and resignation:

you will not leave this place.

In that kitchen she's a girl with a green hair ribbon
staging her innocence before a glass case
of stuffed owls. They beat their wings. She will not
touch the latch. She will not touch

anyone again. The animals revolt.
Mice fight in the walls for territory.
She does not give an inch.

Quickly now, or the latch will lift
before it's over and the animals
will prevent her or wake her children

or drag them in beside the stove.
She hears the scrabbling paws, claws
on the scored lino. She closes
her eyes. The animals gather
around the lake. The lake is on fire.

Art

As Henry James wrote, an artist is one on whom nothing is lost.

Or words approximate to that.

This seems optimistic: it is also true of sustained personal or political cruelty.

A necessary aspect of devotion to another is to not see, to forget, to let go. If nothing were lost, no love would, I think, be practicable.

Under Pinochet's regime, torturers made victims, finally allowed to sleep, keep their hands outside the blankets.

They had thought this through, noticed that it is a small human comfort to curl one's hands under the covers, tucked under the chin or between the legs. Such attention to detail. These were men on whom nothing was lost.

Dutch Masters

1. Adriaen Coorte, Seashells, 1698

Five shells on a slab, scoured clean, no brine
or wobble of flesh, whorls
curiously lit but with
the edge of dark inside. One with spikes like ribs
uncurled from their cage, another lumpy, a cunt
carved out of a potato. The painter
hesitated over his brushes, moved the arrangement
from the table to the window ledge and back to the table,
wanting to render every polished divot,
the ridge like a wave that does not break. He'd ordered
a careful preparation, hoping for a commission
to vault him over his rivals.
Belowstairs, the old woman boiled each one,
jabbed with wire whisks
at the last membranes, lifted her severe cracked finger
to the murky light to marvel at a gobbet clinging there,
last brackish vestige. Her tongue nearly tastes it.

2. Willem Kalf, Still Life with Fruit, Glassware, and a Wanli Bowl, 1659

Empire shorthand: lemons, porcelain,
the fruit on the stem, brittle leaves akimbo. The glass
of pale wine behind the bowl crenulated blue and white,
the black space against which the wine
appears thickened like honey. The lemon,
half-peeled, spongy, hints at desiccation or rot.

I hesitate in the produce aisle, specimens
multiplied by hundreds, the blemished
thrown out, rug vacuumed negligently, bowl
replicated on rows of shelves in Ikea.
Profligate, prophetic, a curse rising
in the oiled dark.

3. Michiel Jansz van Mierevelt, Portrait of Adriana van Ijlen, 1616

Having attained great wealth and great age, she is now free to stare frankly. She has outlived several of her children, her husband, outlived diffidence or flirtation or any burden of pleasure. She is above obligation. Her mouth in a near-smile, cruel as a chisel. Eyes reddened, but not from weeping. She is essentially dry. Her suffering has not widened the scope of her pity. Her pacts with God are private. She does not expect forgiveness.

4. Gerrit Adriaenszoon Berckheyde, Church of Saint Cecilia, Cologne,
about 1670

I could not construct a religion from water,
though it might be stoppered in a poem, any-angled light
congregating in the glass.

Stone will steady you.

These sculpted saints
guarding secrets between pressed palms. Sealed off

from we who are bereft, they are replete, otherwise
we would not need to pray to them.

I sit from time to time in empty churches,
not knowing how to pray. Hoping for belief
the way a tree might for the axe: show me
the pith of my own heart.

Rusalki[2]

We swim in impervious packs, we female suicides, and at death
each receives a head of marvelous red hair we
tangle with the feet of men. Under water, the red
is greenish, like copper. We don't care
what they want. After all, nobody thought
to consider this question in our own cases. But when we leapt,
we leapt freely, drowning with our undesired babies,
husbandly bruises garlanding our throats. In water, the baby
dissolves. Bruises melt like smudges of earth.

We like men very much.
In the depths, we collect them, kiss their faces daily,
polish their startled bared teeth and admire
the washed eyes, bestowing on them the sad smiles of aging fun girls choosing
what to replace youth with, the way you might hesitate in the grocery aisle,
completely at a loss, and though we no longer have this particular problem
we cultivate the sadness. It signals availability
when a man
comes to the river alone,
foolish and cheerful.

Glasses

When I think of Anne Sexton's glasses, I imagine them not on her face but in the collection of the American billionaire who purchased them after she gassed herself in her garage. He keeps them in a temperature-controlled case like an artifact, a page from the King James Bible, a torn strip of papyrus, bitten with hieroglyphs. I saw a photograph of this man once: innocuous, sweating like over-risen dough. Full of unambiguous goodwill, but something else there, something hidden, the way the desert in Texas where he lives might hide things. Does he gloat over the glasses, think about the woman in her car? Does he sometimes, alone, convince himself he sees her eyes in the frames? I imagine he sleeps in a temperature-controlled room, his white bed square and hostile as a glass case.

Jean Grenier[3]

The tremor in my hands is from satisfaction, not hunger.
There is nothing I have not eaten.
Dogs, yes. Cats, yes. Children, yes. See
the yellow of my eyes, smell the reek of me.
I lope behind you on your last road.

Not even the priest can frighten me. Old father, my father
is Lord of the Forest and out of the forest
he came for me, dressed in black and riding a horse
tall as the tower of Saint Michael the Archangel. Gave
me a wolfskin hanging from his saddle. There, he said,
now you know. The villagers put me in this cage

and the monks feed me, but I howl
for my brother-cubs to come to the window
and sing to me when the moon is a swollen eye.
The monks slide the plate across the flagstones
and will not touch me. They let the village girls

admire me as I circle the cage,
nosing my rags into a bed. The kindest
scratch my back with sticks. When I die
the girls will wail out their broken hearts
and toss their cut braids into my grave and the monks
mutter their relief, shamefaced.

The man on the black horse
expects me. I will meet him in the forest.

Mary Shelley at the End of Her Life, Recalling the Monster

I wrote myself into the pristine hysteria of a young woman
that summer when it rained and rained.

Dodged a series of nightmares which sought to swallow me up.
In the end, it was I who ate everything and swelled accordingly.

That summer I was the conduit for the electricity of great men
And conveyed them on their journey toward one another.

I was set at liberty, which meant sitting in a chair waiting for the rain to end.
Neighbours peered with spyglasses, hoping for the great men, who chased

Laudanum visions down the stairs. I dreamed relief: the destruction
Of the drawing rooms and staircases, the great men dashing themselves

On the shoals of their understanding, the afterbirth floating in the chamber
Pot, slopped into a hole by the midwife, earth kicked over it, the treatise

On political economy, religious freedom. The flat gravestone of my mother
That I would lie on, imagining her body under it. But all this was arid.

After so much unhallowed fornication, on gravestones, staircases, braced
Against the backs of chairs, pregnancy made me, I assumed, a woman.

But nothing of womanhood made sense.
What to do with the death I'd birthed?

When I dreamed now
It was of a figure with a face seen only by lightning.

A composition of parts, no more a man
than I was a woman.

It lumbered toward me. The creature had found me out. I thought
We had an understanding but he accused me of carelessness.

My folly as commonplace as the great men's, that I thought
I could draw borders on another, circumscribe a territory

That fitted my dream. He showed me his scars, confessed to standing
At my window, sick with longing. I was taken aback. We took tea.

He held a perfumed handkerchief to his nose. I began to itch in the nethers.
He asked me to dance. When I offered to show him my own stitches

He demurred. Fair enough, I thought, nothing wrong with modesty,
Though I resented, slightly, his more visible seams. Still
We jigged with vigor.

The Light in Vermeer

It pours the way milk pours. The sky hard as porcelain. The woman
reading her letter, instructing her maid. The maid, pouring.

The blue of the sky and the bowl means forgiveness, a hint of Madonna
crouched at the manger. Where is my mother?

A judge in The Hague was asked in the midst of testimony on Bosnia how,
hearing these things, he did not go mad. I look at the Vermeers,

he said. Vermeer would look at the Vermeers. Outside the window
wars of religion, burnt fields, burnt houses, rape. Where did the maid go?

In the next room his violent brother, who attacked his pregnant wife.
The door is closed. The brother does not appear. Here is the room

where these things may not follow. Vermeer made it so he could look
at it. Hard light poured over the water. The blue reminder

that forgiveness must be repeated like housework,
to be undone daily. The maid goes on pouring.

Sixty Harvests

Of Rats and Floods

Rats in the house gnaw basket-straws, cardboard edges, their shit
softening in repeated washings hidden in the fingers of a glove.

Grey stains along the baseboard. They track each other, smelling. Eyes
dried berries. The intelligence of their tails. Whisking, whiskering

and that murmur throughout the night soft as water or the hiss
of gas in the pipes. They are deep inside the house.

I am the tenant to them and they the owners, inheritors. I cannot help
but argue with this in the strident manner of someone who is losing.

My history is a temporary reversal and they know it.
They have no history, only time, which is on their side. I fill the walls

with poisons, sprinkle cloves and oil, barricade myself
with steel wool, witching my incantations. They do not bother

with laughter. It is their indifference I hate. The house softens,
warm and pliant as a cheese, a huge moon-like cheese

they have tunnelled into, not exactly plotting and
I've lost the plot. The house swells. I can feel it shift, lift, it will

not resist, has picked a side and will float away, the rats furrowing
with their outboard motor tails while I'm

on the lawn with a croquet mallet gawking at my mistakenness.
The house, listing as it floats, recedes.

Morecambe Beach

I am told these are among the most dangerous tides in the world.
I come from a country with dangerous tides but

am not familiar with their pull. Not knowing what to avoid,
I pick my way across near the shore, my feet sucked down,

thinking of opaque glass and broken shells. Beneath, I understand,
a murk of ancient vegetation will eat me slowly and without curiosity.

That most human thing, to imagine violent intention
in elemental action. I stoop for a shell. *Cockles and mussels.*

My mother singing in another country. Twenty-one cockle-pickers
imported from China, sent out in the dusk, who did not know

where they were when the tide rose. *Alive, alive-o.* There is a memorial
a little west of here. The last shrimping-boat, docked, is yellow.

Much of the sand on the beach was imported from Romania to address
a sand shortage. The Romanians were also imported, then sent back.

The sand remains, becomes native. There is a tourist shortage. I don't know
what belonging is. Habitation. Habitat. The habit of being

I hope to acquire, as the sand has.

Trying to Explain Time to Children

You will not recognize it. It will feel ordinary.
You will be as you have been:
at a loss and decisive, complete and broken.
You will be sufficient in your lack. You will not get it right.
The time preceding you was also muddied, fraught,
sinful, resolved and cowardly, containing what was not
forgivable yet sometimes forgiven.
You are not singular in your failures.
A woman with varicose veins pisses into a plastic bottle
while on shift in a warehouse
at the same time as your dinner arrives,
as your spoon stirs sugar. Granules
dissolve, the tea amber against the
light, remember that lake we swam in, the water
dark like tea? No, that was before
your birth, and I don't remember either,
I only heard about it. Memory will enclose you
until you can't distinguish between your memories
and others', when you love
them enough to pay attention. Pay attention. As advice goes
it's not what I wanted to give you, I too expected more,
some numinous wisdom, some attainment, not getting by
on slogans and hope, the hunch
that the snarl tightens in one spot as it loosens in another.
The tea is only lukewarm but you drink it.

The Boys Among the Trees

My sons, hiding behind trees,
are rehearsing battle. Secretive
curl of lip, clench of teeth. Faces
among leaves. I walk quickly
the other way, puzzled
by what they think they know.
What I think I know. How we are wrong.

Planetarium

Lie back, she says, flashes
the pointer over us, red incision
in the darkened skyscreen.
I lie back and listen
for my sons' muttering down in the front. My daughter

breathes heavily beside me, watching the laser
indicate we are here as the dome
revolts into stars. Earth's gone,

we're falling. The guide pushes buttons, brightens
the North Star.
We are city people:

humbled by our virtuous awe,
though to be honest I'm comforted
by constellations of electrified houses

even as I anticipate collapse,
people like me befuddled by their uselessness.
The guide, speaking slowly, describes
how the Milky Way and Andromeda galaxies,
expanding toward one another, will

merge. In three billion years, more or less,
there will be two suns in our sky, give or take
a supposition or two, given that nothing
we recognize as consciousness will see it,
given that this place will be a lump
of blackened rock

or something that cannot
be imagined yet.
The thought of this removes
my fear. In the fullness of time, so full

that there are no more days, two suns.
Later, I overhear my older son
tell his friend this news about the suns.
They wish they could see it.

They would live forever
if they could.

Distancing

A man with a dog speaks to me. We have seen the same thing, a framed photograph against a fence beside the garbage can. It is big enough to anchor a room, a family group from the mid–nineteenth century, women flanking the patriarch, faces composed in peevish dignity.

He nudges it with his toe. We allow mild regret, part ways quickly. Though more slowly than we would in ordinary times. The greeting in the street confirms the street is still there.

I'm returning from picking up a pizza where I've asked the owner how business is. *Booming!* he shouts across the counter while I struggle not to touch anything. *Humanity never gives up on life!*

The equation of life with the continued purchase of pizza is comforting. I am comforted by him, a journalist in Albania, now a maker of pizzas. It's patronizing that his hardship reassures me of continuance but I no longer try to suppress it. Every triumphalist cliché is apparently permitted now, any motto or hyperbole. I'm embarrassed by this but carry it back to my children along with the pizza.

There is a painting made in Italy in the fifteenth century attributed to Fra Carnevale, a Dominican monk, called The Ideal City.

White buildings circumscribe a square and a public fountain. While the sky is blue, the unexcitable steady light does not appear to originate from any source. The painting has almost no people in it, like the first photographs centuries later. A few walkers in orderly formation, their faces opaque and rigid as the light.

What is this obedient loneliness?

When I think of modernity I am reluctantly grateful, though I know it's a nebulous formulation, more of a stand-in than a definition.

And yet most of my life is unthinkable without it.

The painting has a prophetic radiance.

Solitude breeds paranoia. That's one of the clichés I'm allowing myself. I do not need to ration them, they will not run out.

Every night I dream of crowds.

Red-footed Tortoise, Science Centre

My daughter believes in this rain forest:
a few feet of water, trees, yellow light
calibrated with shadow. It rains
on cue. She dampens in designed heat,

experiences expected marvels
on the designated path the children run into prosthetic
caves. The stone yields to their hands, a delight
of fear without a sequel, wildness
cut down to manageable size. Nothing here

is grander than themselves. The tortoise, glass-boxed,
heaves from corner to corner as if the earth
could be reduced to this. As if we could be forgiven.

Hags

Relieved, we returned to the manufacture and sale of small plastic objects.
What had been horror became normalcy and what we abhorred

We longed for, a sign we still possessed what passed
For the substance of our lives. I hurry

Toward ephemera strewn on metal shelves, the promise
Of delight for my children. The old woman at the cash attempts, I think,

A smile above the mask line. I smile back, lick absently
At the lining of my own. Blush at the texture of cloth on tongue.

My neighbours fight with one another. Three generations
Grown in one bungalow, no murder yet. The grandmother

Who once climbed her roof to attack a raccoon with a broom,
Who hands stiff bread to me over our fence, is thrust

Out the back door into the yard. Her grey face
Squat and neutral as a risen loaf. Behind the door

Her daughter wails, her son-in-law, who rarely speaks, shouts
Monster monster through the screen. She sits on the step

With her wheeled shopping cart, but the yard
Can only be exited through the house. Sobs

From the kitchen, more shouting (the husband, I think)
At her through the screen. She settles like sand

At the bottom of a jar. Tucks her knees up. Spying
From the bathroom window I see or guess at

A perplexed satisfaction in her face, a glint
Of goblin malice at the howl at her back, she's

The weather maker and the storm's eye, Baba Yaga
In her chicken-leg hut gnawing long bones.

I duck, afraid of being seen, afraid
the word that finds her there is right.

Original daub on the streaming wall, old woman
Slurping soup at the back of the cave swollen with dark.

Sixty Harvests

The man on the radio says sixty harvests. Sixty harvests
until there are no more. My eldest will be
the same age as my mother. Sixty harvests
and I wonder if they can mulch my body into
a wheat field. Drive your cart and your plow over
the bones of the dead. My children run in from the street
gobbling fruit, my children ride bicycles in the yard
of their school to which they walk each morning,
my children are the lucky ones, sixty harvests.
The afternoon light looks very much like
other afternoons in early fall. I write
a grocery list, meet a friend for a drink, realize
that I expect a reward at some point, at which
my life will achieve the burnish of art, hard
and compact as a jewel, that I am waiting for
my own arrival. Sixty harvests. My daughter
sews masks at the sewing machine while my sons
fight each other while three men who have bought
the house next door struggle with drywall and smoke
companionably in the front yard. My wife and I
are easy with each other, then uneasy, then easy again.
We are low on milk. Late at night
some boys set off fireworks on the train tracks
and then it thunders. My youngest is afraid of the dark.
He likes a series of books about mice in eighteenth-century
farmhouses. In the morning, the rain
causes me to cancel a series of small plans. My children
sit on the couch, dishes sit in the sink, pots on the stove,
the men next door bark, I ask my neighbour for milk,
accompany another neighbour to the park, hang
socks on the line, the radio is still on,
the milk spills, the shirt I intended to wear is
cat-haired, I fret about political differences so slight
they amount to points of etiquette and that my
humiliations trouble me more than my sins, my children

outgrow their clothes, my wife bakes bread,
and sixty harvests, sixty harvests, sixty harvests.

I look up from the line. Above me the geese
in formation cry their way home.

A Conversation

I know something, my son says. He refers,
in confidence, to the book we have just read. Flips between
the pages, which shine like raw eggs. *See?* The mother
who sends the children into the woods and the witch
entrenched in her candy house (the pages fold
under his hands)—he is trying to make me understand.
What? I ask, the abstracted edge creeping in.
He waits. What? What? (that tone comes on so quickly)
He points. *I know that the witch and the mother are the same.*
No. No. No. I try not to hurt his feelings, to explain
it's only the style of their headdresses. My refutation
becomes a special pleading. He is stern, taking
the book into his lap. He understands.

Mishima and the Park Bench

Say attention is repetition.

Most things are repetition.

Religion, love.

Forgiveness.

Housework.

Children, marriage.

The meal, the congealed scraps, the bedtime, sleep.

The house, which repeats itself like a stammered word never completed, lives jammed into it over and over, before you, after you.

The old woman who lived here before us returned from the repetition of grocery shopping, sat in her kitchen chair, lit a cigarette, died. I don't know, as my neighbours who told me this don't know, if she was able to inhale, but I like to think of her on the chair, smoke thoughtfully about her head,

deep in the burden of familiarity before her body bucked her out into that irreducible unknown thing.

Once and once only.

I doubt I will be lucky enough to die like that.

Before I understood my life to be a series of grooves worn shallowly into a small piece of stone, I sat on a park bench weeping from a broken heart and reading Yukio Mishima and smoking until I threw up in the grass.

There was, I think, a grey and white picture of a mask on the cover, an image that had nothing to do with the book.

I remember a group of patrician old women in one of the stories whose lifelong friendship ends over a foolish dispute about a ring. I was too young to experience the story as a tragedy, and the author disliked women too much to see it that way either, so no one is left to see it that way in this particular grouping, except the women themselves, who do not exist.

But the point is the park bench and the wet grass and my conviction regarding the truth of loneliness.

My broken heart was, I imagined, a singular event. There could be only one. There could only be room for one.

This was the condition of my loneliness. Something like an egg laid gently in a pot of boiling water, pure because it never engenders anything.

I intended to be someone who wept on benches at dusk in empty parks, reading. Self-important in my misery.

Later, I discovered brokenheartedness to be in fact a repetition, small fractures daily. The way I crumble bits of shell into the compost in the morning, carefully crushing because I have told my children about witches and their boats and now they watch me do it, assured that I know what's right.

Grey cracks along the shell like the plaster of an old house.

To have children is to be brokenhearted so often it is not worth mentioning.

So much of life is not worth mentioning. But I mention it anyway. I can't seem to help it.

It is commonplace to note the centrality of forgiveness in marriage. So commonplace it seems not worth mentioning until you realize that forgiveness is not a singular act but a habit, not perfected but repeated imperfectly until the groove is worn in the stone.

As my children grow into themselves I think of their patrimony of plastic and dirty water and do not think they will forgive us. They will not have time to form the habit.

But I've been wrong before and been forgiven.

Semi-lockdown

Because poetry makes nothing happen, we sat by the river. We had been told
to shelter in place, except for those who had no shelter.

Silent, we sat by the river, which ran on. We were all in this
together but some more so than others.

There'll be stars in your crown. A saying frequently invoked by the woman
who married my grandfather, and placed great stock in obedience.

She used to make a rubbing motion with her left fingers. She did not know
this—she was viciously unselfconscious in most things.

When she died I inherited the gesture. This interested me as I did not like
her and we were not blood relations.

I am not related to my children by blood. This shows blood's comparative
unimportance to love, though I am not related by blood to strangers,

many of whom have no shelter, but this does not trouble my blood
as much as I hoped it would when, younger,

I thought of myself. This is not a new problem,
the blood problem.

Two of my children sleep late. One wakes early, dresses quietly,
bikes out into the morning light.

A poet reminds me that I am not hungry. I eat rapaciously, and well
into the evening. The river ran on.

Sometimes my son does not get home until dark. The sky opens, beautiful
as a bruise. I look out the skylight at the houses.

My son returns, impatient with me. This is in some way an impatience with interpretation. He senses I wish to interpret him.

When I hear him go, I practice. This is what I tell myself, that I am practicing. I am practicing letting him go.

Lent

Lent

1.

The lake has a provisional name. It's been known by other names, and possibly those names were also in some way provisional. The lake may have a name for itself.

Beside the lake, it seems feasible to believe that this is not just pathetic fallacy, that the lake really does have a name it has given itself, that it keeps secret. It keeps things.

My friend, kneeling on the sand, arranged stones in a circle as she told me about the dreams by which she commemorates her dead.

The lake has eaten the stones.

2.

There were people in the church today and I went in. I like the melancholy of churches. There is a spaciousness in failure. The minister, breaking the bread, wears a small smile that suggests he knows the futility of what he does and does it anyway, out of love, out of habit, the way the two are, over time, indistinguishable.

I love because I have grown the habit of love. I cannot love all at once, by will or by choice. It happens gradually, like water overtaking the shore. Slowly, without noticing, the shoreline alters. I suppose that is what this man might mean by grace.

I was not raised in churches, for the usual reasons. I am ambivalent about this, but would rather ambivalence than certainty, given the history of certainty. I will live ambivalently, which is a pretty meagre supper, not much more than a self-regarding gruel, perhaps an excuse for evading the problem of evil, or the other problem, of good, by not quite believing in either one. By not quite believing but longing for belief. At eighteen I walked out of a church in Italy into the square where a group of boys played soccer and I knew God was real in the blunt humiliation of that statement.

But then my life went on as before, God just another metaphor.

And maybe God was present only because I was a tourist, the boys and the thousand-year-old paving stones placed there so that I might find them and be transfigured, while they (the boys, the stones) remained luminously flat, without fault or flaw, without meaning except for mine.

3.

My father, as a boy, heard a sermon in which the minister told the congregation that they must pray unceasingly. He was a serious child with no mother, not because his mother was dead but because she had left, not because she had left but because she was sent by his father back to the country where she was born. Boys belong to fathers. She was not permitted to say goodbye. He came home and his mother wasn't there.

The few times I met her, when I was a child, she was like a moth burning itself on a light bulb, fluttering around him, not knowing what to do now that he was a man and she was old.

My father snuck back into the church later on to begin his career in unceasing prayer. He knelt. Someone came in. Embarrassed, he lay on the floor and hid.

O Lord hear our prayer
And may our cry come unto thee

When I think of God I think of the way a child hides. In hope of being found.

4.

This church, St. Andrews by the Lake, is nearly empty. There is a table in the aisle and a tray of pebbles. We are asked to remember our dead by dropping the stones into a dish of water. I hold my stones until they are warmed. They darken as they sink.

5.

On Ash Wednesday, the first day of Lent, the priest makes the sign of the cross on the believer's forehead with ash, saying *remember you are dust and to dust you shall return*. Originally only women's foreheads were marked and men's hair scattered with ash like billows of smoke from a small fire. Women were required to cover their heads in church.

Remember you are dust and to dust you shall return is a modern formulation, replacing *Remember, man, that thou art dust, and to dust thou shalt return* spoken to Adam and Eve in the garden before they were turned out of the gates and started walking, and they've been walking ever since.

What you are, we were. What we are, you will be.

I don't believe Adam walked with God in the cool of the evening. The heart has always hankered after imaginary gardens, and no one has ever marked my forehead with ash, but I long for it as something that would set a limit on time, the motion of the finger, the blessing that does not lie. So much of living seems like a fraudulent immortality, a profane falsehood, and I want someone to tell me that I was once something else and will be again.

I don't want this very sincerely.

Or only in the way I want experience to be unified, a guilty secret, a totalitarian desire. It might be better, in the sense of very slightly less reprehensible, to be fraudulent and broken, though I'm not sure how much better. This might be a way of comforting myself, wistfully defending the beleaguered corner of people who suspect that we are not made to be whole.

6.

My friend is fretting over the profusion of her father's books. Her father must move to a retirement home, partly for the sake of his wife. He is 92, and swims every day. He fled the Iranian Revolution along with his wife and daughters when my friend was a child. She has never returned, though she has seen in pictures the house of her earliest childhood standing uninhabited, orphaned in a street where every other house has been replaced by concrete slabs of apartment blocks. Her father, a civil servant and then a security guard, has read devotedly all his life, but it's only my conjecture that reading has provided him with the solace of unlived lives, a consolation, a home.

His books number in the thousands. Eighteenth-century love poetry, illegally distributed Marxist theory from the 70s collected at enormous risk to himself and his family, books of Persian history. *I don't even read Farsi anymore, not really, not at that level*, my friend says, *and who will want these books, who will read them now?* There is a fragile pause between us before the optimistic swerve: university libraries, history departments, the young academic who hungers for those illegal pamphlets, some place where the love her father gave these books will not be wasted, as if it is not the nature of love to be wasted. But there's the pause, wondering what should be done with the past.

We smile at each other bleakly. Nothing can be done. To preserve the entirety of the past you would need to let it crush you.

We keep smiling. Decent, conscientious. Not willing to be obliterated.

7.

Bristlecone pines grow along arid mountain ridges and can live to be 5,000 years old. They are squat, twisted. Survivors, not conquerors. As secret as the lake.

In 1967, a graduate student in Arizona wished to cut down what he believed to be the oldest example of this tree in order to count the rings. He summoned a forester. The man laid his hand on the trunk and said to the student *I will not touch this tree*. The young man found another forester who cut down the tree for him.

This is a story about the uselessness of sanctity: the first forester could not save the tree. But I hope it can stand as an epitaph. I think there would be no better way to be remembered.

To have said *I will not touch this tree*.

8.

I, of course, do not understand quantum mechanics. Niels Bohr, addressing an audience of philosophers, expressed disappointment, even anger, when the philosophers listened to his findings stolidly, with impassive faces. *If a man does not feel dizzy*, he said, *then he has not understood a word.*

As I tentatively understand it:

Everything that could possibly happen has already happened, and we only noticed part of it.

This statement makes instinctual sense to me, though I cannot understand it literally any more than I can understand God this way. My undisciplined hope is that it is a form of poetry, meaning it works on a hunch, what cannot be said but only indicated, what is outside the possibilities of the literal.

9.

Might the world offer a way out of the world? A river? A door? Is this a
rhetorical question?

10

I was introduced to the work of the Expressionist painter Charlotte Salomon through a series of panels painted on cardboard squares torn from grocery delivery boxes and arranged along one wall of a barn in Vermont. The series is entitled *Let Us Praise the Wondrous Life of Charlotte Salomon* and painted in the style of medieval religious paintings and also in the style of Salomon and also in the style of the old man who painted them, who lives near the barn.

He makes cardboard testaments to things that might be remembered for a while.

Not permanently. Just for a while.

The barn is very dry, as is the art within it. One spark, and it would go. This does not trouble him. Let it burn, he said. *The burdens of history are already over-plentiful.* Let something exist for a while and be forgotten and make room.

Having spent a little time with this man, I don't believe he's lying. He does not wish to inflict a permanent mark on the world. He is reconciled with being. Not guarded against the fire. He has laid himself down.

11.

Just before Charlotte Salomon, who was five months pregnant, was gassed at Auschwitz, a witness claims she saw the sky and cried out *God my God how beautiful it is!*

There is nothing to be gleaned from this. But I do want it to stand. So I'll write it down, and see what follows.

Though the circumstances make me wary of meaning.

And yet.

A talismanic hope that it might be possible to notice that the sky is still there?

That we are a form of praise?

12.

God my God, how beautiful it is.

Endnotes

1. Assia Wevill was the partner of Ted Hughes toward the end of Sylvia Plath's life and after her death. Wevill committed suicide by the same method along with her young daughter in 1969.
2. Rusalki are mermaid-like creatures in Slavic folklore. They are spirits of women who drowned themselves to escape violent marriages or unwanted pregnancies, and they lure men into the river to drown them.
3. Jean Grenier was a teenager who confessed to a series of murders in France in the early 1600s, claiming he was a werewolf. He was sent to live with the Franciscan friars in Bordeaux, and he died there in 1611.

Acknowledgements

Some of these poems previously appeared, in different forms and sometimes under different titles, in *The Ampersand Review*, *The Antigonish Review*, *Arc*, *ArtsEverywhere*, *Carousel*, *CV2*, *The Dalhousie Review*, *The Fiddlehead*, *Grain*, *Image*, and *Plenitude Magazine*. Thanks to the editors.

"Morecambe Beach" was written while working with Zuppa Theatre in collaboration with Lancaster Arts, in Morecambe, UK. Thanks to everyone who told me stories.

The title poem won the 2021 Ross and Davis Mitchell Prize for Faith and Poetry, judged by Shane McCrae, Suzanne Buffam, and Liz Howard, and administered by Lisa Ann Cockrel. Many thanks.

"Mary Shelley at the End of Her Life, Recalling the Monster," is for Ker Wells (1964-2019), and was drawn from writing he commissioned from me as part of a project at Simon Fraser University, which was never completed, and which I have repurposed, with thanks to his memory.

Thank you also to Ladan Behbin, David Cayley, Jessica Moore, and Peter Schumann of the Bread and Puppet Theater, for their appearance in "Lent."

Work on this collection was supported at times by the Canada Council for the Arts and the Ontario Arts Council. Without this support, it might not have ever been finished.

Thank you to Jay and Hazel MillAr and everyone at Book*hug for giving this book such a fine home. Thank you to Karen Solie, an editor who pushed me harder in a spirit of rigour and goodwill. Thank you Michel Vrana for the cover. I'm blessed.

Thank you to the Toronto Public Library, where I was writer in residence while working on the manuscript, and especially Cameron Ray for his work facilitating the residency.

Thank you to Peter Wills for graciously maintaining my website.

Thank you to my parents, David Cayley and Jutta Mason.

Thank you to my friends.

Thank you to Lea Ambros and our children, Livia, Tom, and Danny. You're the best.

About the Author

Kate Cayley is the author of two previous poetry collections, a young adult novel, and two short story collections, including *How You Were Born*, winner of the Trillium Book Award and shortlisted for the Governor General's Literary Award for Fiction. A tenth anniversary edition of *How You Were Born* is forthcoming from Book*hug Press in 2024. She has also written several plays which have been performed in Canada, the US, and the UK, and is a frequent writing collaborator with the immersive company Zuppa Theatre. Cayley has won the O. Henry Short Story Prize, the *PRISM International* Short Fiction Prize, the Geoffrey Bilson Award for Historical Fiction, and a Chalmers Fellowship. She has been a finalist for the K. M. Hunter Award, the Carter V. Cooper Short Story Prize, and the Toronto Arts Foundation Emerging Artist Award, and longlisted for the Frank O'Connor International Short Story Prize, and the CBC Literary Prizes in both poetry and fiction. In 2021, she won the Mitchell Prize for Faith and Poetry for the title poem in *Lent*. Cayley lives in Toronto with her wife and their three children.

Colophon

Manufactured as the first edition of
Lent
in the spring of 2023 by Book*hug Press

Edited for the press by Karen Solie
Copy edited by Andrea Waters
Proofread by Charlene Chow
Type + design by Michel Vrana
Cover photo by Addictive Stock / photocase.com

Printed in Canada

bookhugpress.ca